WEIRD ROCKS

Michele Corriel

ILLUSTRATED BY
Dan Bilyeu

2013
Mountain Press Publishing Company
Missoula, Montana

For Pat — Thank you for sharing your world and making me a "Junior Geologist."
I love every minute of it, even when you load up my backpack with rocks. — M. C.

*To good friends and family who have encouraged me and had faith in me. —*D. B.

© 2013 by Michele Corriel
First Printing, January 2013
All rights reserved

Illustrations © 2013 by Dan Bilyeu
Photographs by Tom Ferris

Library of Congress Cataloging-in-Publication Data

Corriel, Michele.
Weird rocks / Michele Corriel ; illustrated by Dan Bilyeu.
  pages cm
 ISBN 978-0-87842-597-6 (cloth : alk. paper)
 1. Rocks–Juvenile literature. 2. Minerals–Juvenile literature. I. Bilyeu, Dan, 1955- illustrator. II. Title.
 QE432.2.C67 2013
 552–dc23

                              2012030634

Printed in Hong Kong

MP Mountain Press
PUBLISHING COMPANY
P.O. Box 2399 • Missoula, MT 59806 • 406-728-1900
800-234-5308 • info@mtnpress.com
www.mountain-press.com

WEIRD ROCKS

Do you look for colorful rocks, smooth rocks, striped rocks, or flat rocks for skipping across a pond? Do you ever pick up rocks full of shiny crystals and wonder what they are made of? If so, you may be a rock hound, and this book is for you.

In these pages, you'll learn all about rocks that do amazing things, from rocks you can use to write on the sidewalk to rocks that float on water, and from rocks that burn like wood to rocks that travel through space.

Rocks are made of minerals. If you think of a rock as a building, minerals are like bricks. There are nearly 5,000 kinds of minerals in the world of all different colors, sizes, shapes, and textures. These different minerals combine in different ways to make every rock unique. And, as you will discover, some rocks are just plain weird.

I wrote this book to share with you the secrets behind the strangest rocks I know. I hope that reading it will make you want to go outside and find some weird rocks of your own!

ROCKS THAT FLOAT

Don't you think it's weird that a rock the size of a baseball can float in water? A rock called *pumice* does just that. It looks like a sponge and has lots of holes full of air. Pumice forms when hot lava spews out of a volcano and cools quickly, trapping air bubbles inside. Bubbles near the rock's surface pop, leaving behind tiny holes you can see. More air holes are hidden inside the rock. Pumice is lightweight and floats because of all the air bubbles still trapped inside it. You could make your friends think you're a superhero by lifting a huge piece of it!

Each tiny hole in these pieces of pumice is about the size of a grain of sand.

ROCKS THAT APPEAR LIKE MONSTERS

Don't you think it's weird that rocks can rise out of a lake like the Creature from the Black Lagoon? In Mono Lake, California, calcium-rich springwater bubbles up from below. A rock called *tufa,* which is made up of calcium carbonate, is deposited around the underwater spring. As layer after layer is added, a mound of tufa grows upward from the bottom of the lake. The city of Los Angeles began taking water from streams entering Mono Lake in 1941, causing the lake level to drop. As the water level fell, the tufa towers began to appear above the water. What do you imagine people thought was coming out of the lake?

ROCKS THAT ATTRACT

Don't you think it's weird that a rock can attract metal like a magnet? A mineral called *magnetite* does just that. Small grains of magnetite occur in rocks cooled from hot lava. Made mostly of iron, this mineral is one of Earth's few natural magnets. Legend has it that Magnes, a Greek shepherd, discovered the mineral when he noticed that the nails in his shoes were clinging to the rock. What else would stick to a piece of magnetite?

Crystals of magnetite look like shiny metallic cubes, but they have eight sides instead of six.

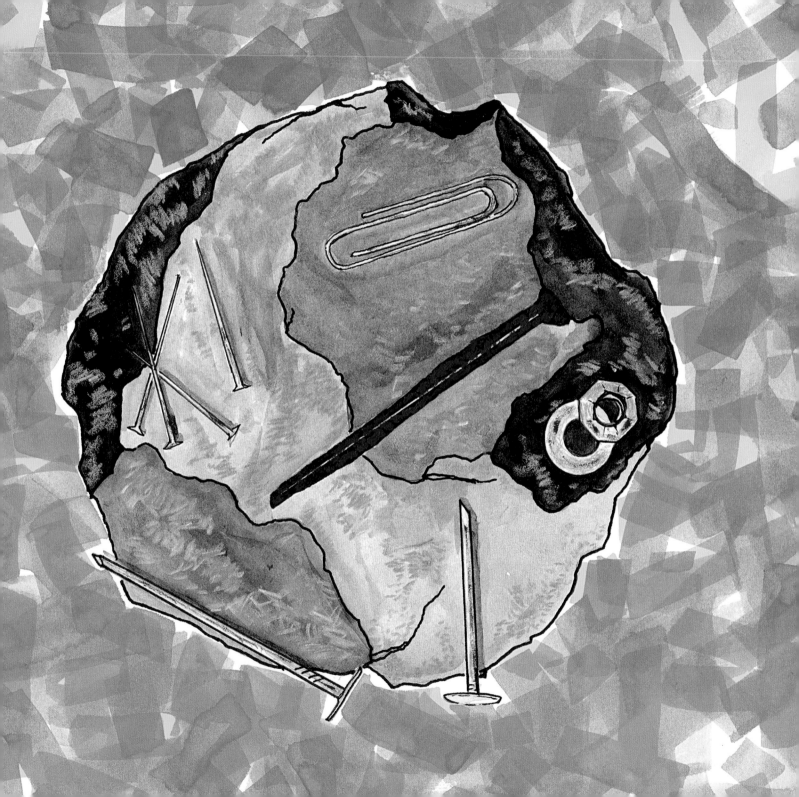

ROCKS THAT BURN

Don't you think it's weird that a rock can catch fire as if it were a piece of wood or a pile of dry leaves? *Coal* and *oil shale* do just that because they contain the element carbon—the same substance that burns in wood. These two weird rocks are made of the remains of ancient plants and animals, so they are called fossil fuels. Wildfires started by lightning have set hillsides of coal on fire in Colorado, North Dakota, and other places. Would you roast a hot dog over one of those fires?

Oil shale smells sort of like engine oil.

ROCKS WITH HIDDEN TREASURE

Rock collectors split geodes in half with special rock saws.

Don't you think it's weird that a plain-looking rock can be full of beautiful crystals? You won't find treasures in just any rock—it has to be a *geode*. They form when water deposits minerals in holes in rocks. Much later, wind and rain can wear away the softer surrounding rock, exposing the round, hard mass of minerals. Geodes look dull on the outside but have colorful crystals of quartz, calcite, fluorite, and other minerals on the inside.

Got your hammer, Matey?

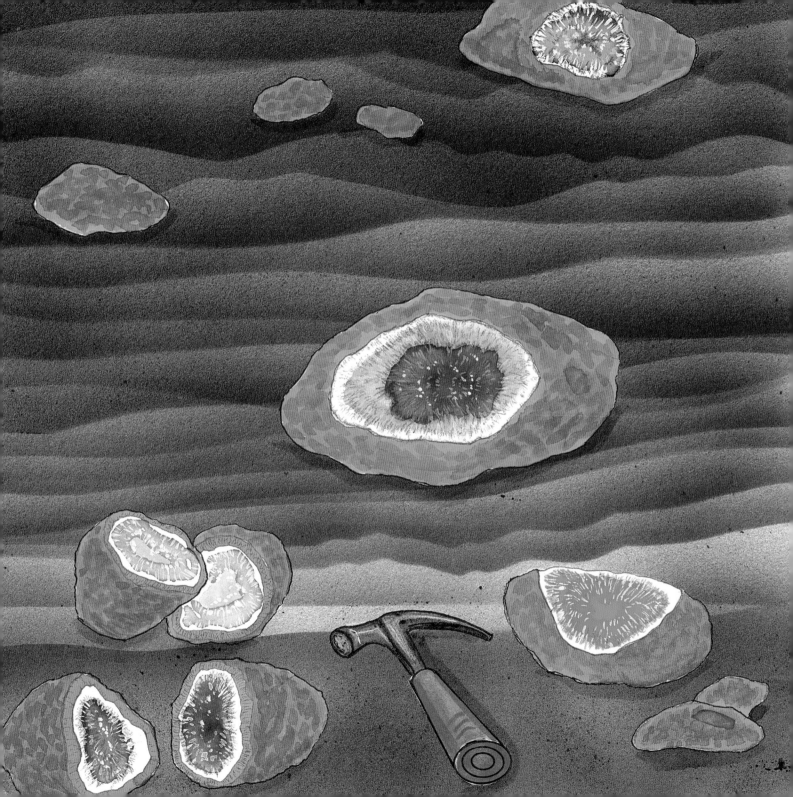

ROCKS THAT GLOW

Don't you think it's weird that a rock can glow in the dark like a lightbulb? A mineral called *scheelite* glows bright blue under ultraviolet light. In regular daylight, scheelite looks similar to many other minerals, making it difficult to find. During World War II, the United States wanted to find scheelite because it contains tungsten, a very hard metal used to make weapons. Ultraviolet lamps were attached to the blades of bulldozers to make scheelite easier to spot. That must have been a freaky sight!

Scheelite doesn't glow in normal light.

ROCKS THAT STINK

Don't you think it's weird that a rock can smell like a rotten egg? A lemon yellow mineral called *sulfur* does just that. Sulfur gas is what makes rotten eggs stink. This sulfur gas is also responsible for the strong smell you'll encounter at volcanic areas such as Yellowstone National Park. The mineral sulfur is often found coating volcanic rocks. The smell would make a skunk hold its nose!

It's a good thing this isn't a scratch-and-sniff book.

ROCKS THAT SAIL

Don't you think it's weird that a rock can move across a flat plain as if it had a sail? On a dry lakebed in Death Valley, in the desert of California, people discovered tracks left by rocks. Some of these tracks were nearly 2,000 feet long. It was clear that the rocks originally fell from the steep mountains at one end of the lakebed, but it took scientists quite a while to figure out how they got to the middle of the lakebed. It rarely rains in that area, but when it does, the lakebed gets slick. If the wind blows really hard when the lakebed is wet, the rocks move. The flat plain has no vegetation, so wind gusts can reach 90 miles per hour. That would make a rock sail!

ROCKS THAT WRITE

Don't you think it's weird that you can write with a rock? A white rock called *chalk* looks, feels, and writes just like the chalk used on blackboards and sidewalks. Flecks of this soft rock break off when you drag it across a hard surface. Tall white cliffs along England's seacoast, known as the White Cliffs of Dover, are made of chalk. It formed underwater millions of year ago, when small particles shed by tiny algae settled to the bottom of an ancient sea. If you find a chalky-looking rock, try writing with it. If it makes a mark, you won't have to buy chalk at the store!

Chalk is white and is made up of very tiny particles.

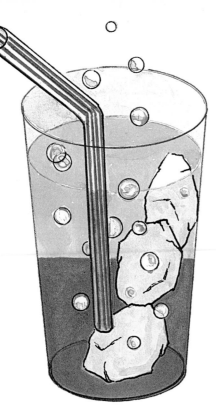

ROCKS THAT FIZZ

Don't you think it's weird that a rock can fizz like a glass of soda? A rock called *limestone* does just that if you put a drop of acid on it. Limestone is made of calcium carbonate, usually from the shells and skeletons of sea creatures.

When acid contacts calcium carbonate, carbon dioxide is released, the same gas that bubbles up out of a carbonated soda. When in the field, geologists often carry a small bottle of acid in their pack to help identify limestone. If limestone fizzed in water, you could make a bubbly drink with it!

Do you see the fossil in this piece of limestone?

ROCKS FROM SPACE

Don't you think it's weird that a rock can fly through space like a rocket ship and land on Earth? It happens all the time. When a rock from space enters the air surrounding Earth, it starts to burn, creating a fireball. If it doesn't burn up completely, it lands on Earth and is called a *meteorite*. Most meteorites are pretty small. But sometimes huge ones crash into Earth, creating gigantic holes in the ground. A large meteorite hit the desert floor in Arizona more than 20,000 years ago and made a hole 700 feet deep and 4,000 feet across. Watch out for flying rocks!

A meteorite will have a smooth, pitted surface if it began to melt when it was still a fireball.

ROCKS MADE OF POOP

Most coprolites don't look anything like poop.

Don't you think it's weird that rocks can form from old poop? But that's exactly how rocks called *coprolites* are made. When dinosaurs roamed the Earth, they ate and then pooped, just like animals do today. Most of the poop turned into soil, but some was covered by mud and other sediment and was preserved. Over time, minerals replace the buried poop, changing it to rock. Sometimes dinosaur poop was enormous. While digging up some *Tyrannosaurus rex* fossils in Canada, scientists found a coprolite that was 17 inches long, 6 inches high, and 5 inches wide. Now that would plug up a toilet!

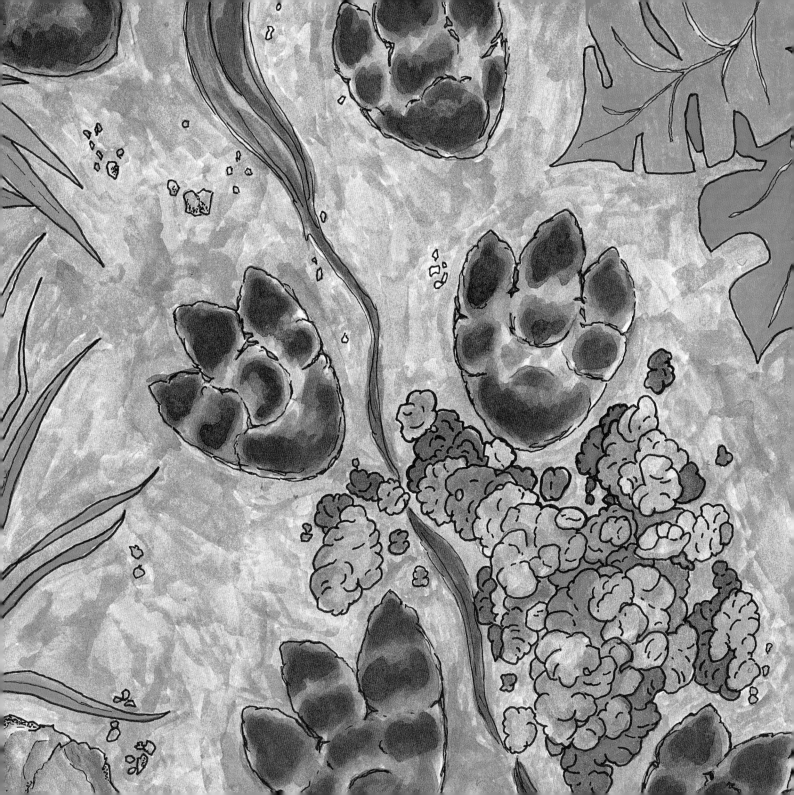

ROCKS THAT CUT

Don't you think it's weird that a rock can be as sharp as a piece of broken glass? In fact, a rock called *obsidian* is exactly that—glass. When hot lava explodes from a volcano, sometimes it cools so fast that there isn't time for minerals to form. The lava freezes into glass almost instantly. Historically, obsidian was an important stone to primitive peoples because it cuts so well. They made it into arrow points, knives, and other tools. Some researchers say that obsidian makes a cleaner cut than the sharpest metal knife!

Obsidian is so shiny that you can see your reflection in it, like a mirror.

ROCKS THAT RING

Don't you think it's weird that a rock can ring like a bell? On a mountain in Montana and at Ringing Rocks Park in Pennsylvania, there are fields of large rocks that ring when they are hit with a hammer or another rock. The sound is different for each rock. Sometimes it's a high-pitched ding, sometimes a dull chime. The strangest thing about these rocks is that no one knows why they make musical sounds. Some scientists suspect it's because the rocks, which cooled deep inside the Earth from hot magma, contain a lot of iron, a metal often used to make bells. Ringing rocks occur at only a few other places in the world. You could hold a real rock concert at one of these sites!

ROCKS THAT FOOL

Do you see the grain of the wood in this petrified wood?

Don't you think it's weird that a rock can look just like wood? Most wood rots after a tree dies, but sometimes entire logs become rocks, a rare find called *petrified wood*. Wood won't rot if it's buried in something that prevents air from reaching it. Sometimes a volcanic eruption buries a tree or an entire forest in hot ash. Sometimes a flood or landslide buries logs in mud. Water seeping through the ground slowly replaces the buried wood with minerals, changing it to rock. You can still see the patterns of the grain of the wood, tree rings, and bark in petrified wood. Do you think a woodpecker would be fooled?

ROCKS THAT CHANGE COLOR

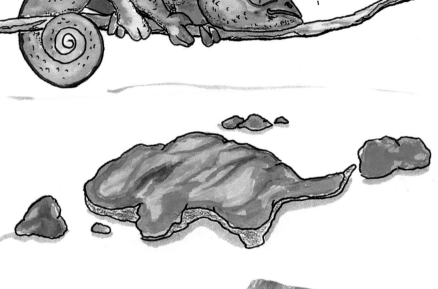

Don't you think it's weird that a rock can change color like a chameleon? The mineral *labradorite* does just that, especially when it's polished for jewelry. If you hold it up to the light, the bluish green surface shimmers and changes colors, kind of like a butterfly's wings. When labradorite forms deep beneath the surface of the Earth, two parts of its crystal crisscross. When light bounces back and forth within the crystal, you may see blues and violets or greens, yellows, and oranges.

Labradorite is a type of feldspar, a mineral with a boxy shape.

ABOUT THE AUTHOR

Michele Corriel is a children's book author and freelance writer living and working in Belgrade, Montana. Her work has taken her from the art galleries of New York City to the back roads of the Rockies. Her middle-grade novels include *Fairview Felines: A Newspaper Mystery* and *True Lies: A Newspaper Mystery*. When she's not out rockhounding with Pat, her husband and favorite geologist, she's probably got her nose in a good book.

ABOUT THE ILLUSTRATOR

Dan Bilyeu lives in Bozeman, Montana, with his dog, Carmel O'Pup; his partner, Stacy Jackson; and her dog The Mighty Fly. He received a degree in art and graphic design in 1995 from Montana State University at Bozeman and has always been interested in illustration and design of everything from architecture to type. Dan spends his spare time rolling around in vintage cars, owning (though not mastering) many different guitars, and enjoying Montana, a beautiful place to live.